Clever Puzzles for Brainy Kids

Sterling Publishing Co., Inc.
New York

Puzzles by Friederike Barnhusen and Christiane Krapp
Illustrations by Bianca Peters

10 9 8 7 6 5 4 3 2

Published by Sterling Publishing Co., Inc.
387 Park Avenue South, New York, N.Y. 10016
Excerpted from the books *Gehirnjogging für Kinder 1.Klasse;*
Gehirnjogging für Kinder 2. Klasse; Gehirnjogging für Kinder
3. Klasse © 2001 Edition Bucherbar im Arena Verlag GmbH.
English translation © 2003 by Sterling Publishing Co., Inc.
Distributed in Canada by Sterling Publishing
c/o Canadian Manda Group, One Atlantic Avenue, Suite 105
Toronto, Ontario, Canada M6K 3E7
Distributed in Great Britain and Europe by Chris Lloyd at Orca Book
Services, Stanley House, Fleets Lane, Poole BH15 3AJ, England
Distributed in Australia by Capricorn Link (Australia) Pty Ltd.
P.O. Box 704, Windsor, NSW 2756, Australia

Sterling ISBN 1-4027-0550-6

Dear Parents:

School and everyday life demand a multitude of mental abilities from children. In sports it goes without saying that the body must be trained. But a targeted training is also imperative for the mind in order to meet all these mental demands. The puzzles in this book have been designed to build up the ability to think, independent of any educational pedagogy and classroom content.

Based on the newest developments in intelligence psychology and brain research, these exercises do not follow any specific learning strategy but rather develop the basic mental efficiency of the child. Through training the brain, learning is generally made easier. Many exercises lend themselves well to repetition and the incentive is, as with any other kind of training, a sense of achievement.

The exercises are fun and stimulate important brain functions:

- Visual perception
- Memory
- Quick understanding
- The ability to recognize connections
- The ability to draw the right conclusion

Explanations

The first tasks are kept simple to guarantee an effortless entry into the exercises. The instructions are deliberately short and formulated concisely so that the child can work with the book even without outside help. Answers are in the back, so the child can feel the satisfaction of verifying his or her success.

As you would with physical training, you can also keep track of the child's progress with these techniques. After some practice, the child's success becomes visible here as well. In one exercise, the child grasps the principles required to perform the first task. Compare the time it takes for the first task with the time of the challenges that follow! And the child will become comfortable using many of these techniques in the standardized tests that he or she will take later on.

In most cases, a soft pencil is all you need to solve the tasks. For others, colored pencils or crayons will help. These exercises may be repeated as often as you like. Every time they are performed, the puzzles will be solved faster and more easily.

Friederike Barnhusen and Christiane Krapp

Funny Masks

Every colored mask on this page has a black-and-white twin. Find the twins and write the number of the colored mask in the small box above each one.

A Great Outfit

There are lots of different shapes in this outfit — circles, triangles, rectangles, and ovals.
How many circles can you find? Circle the box that has the right number of circles.

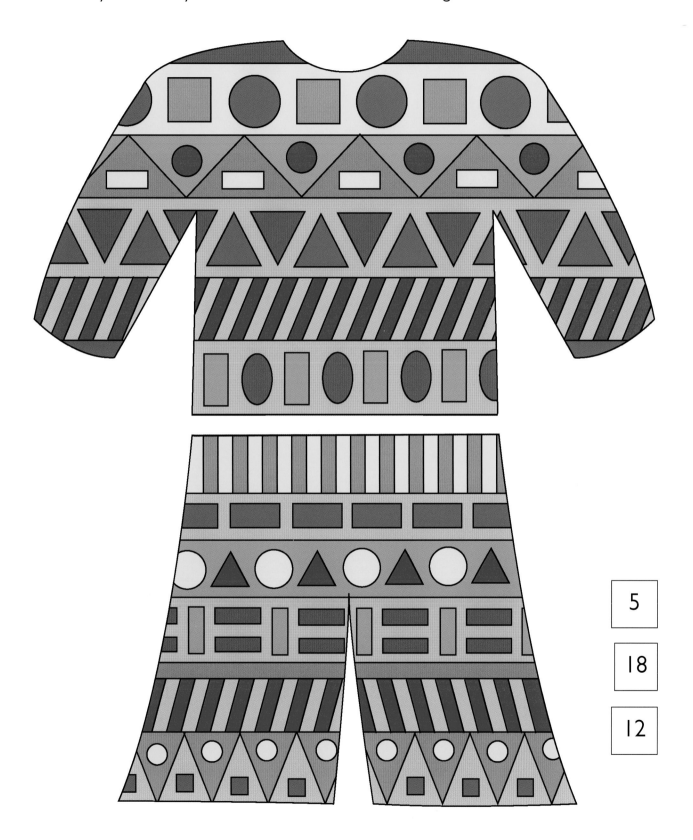

5

18

12

The Eagle Family

You can find the eagle in the square a few times on these pages. How many can you find?

Green Crocodiles

How many green crocodiles do you see? Circle the box with the right number.

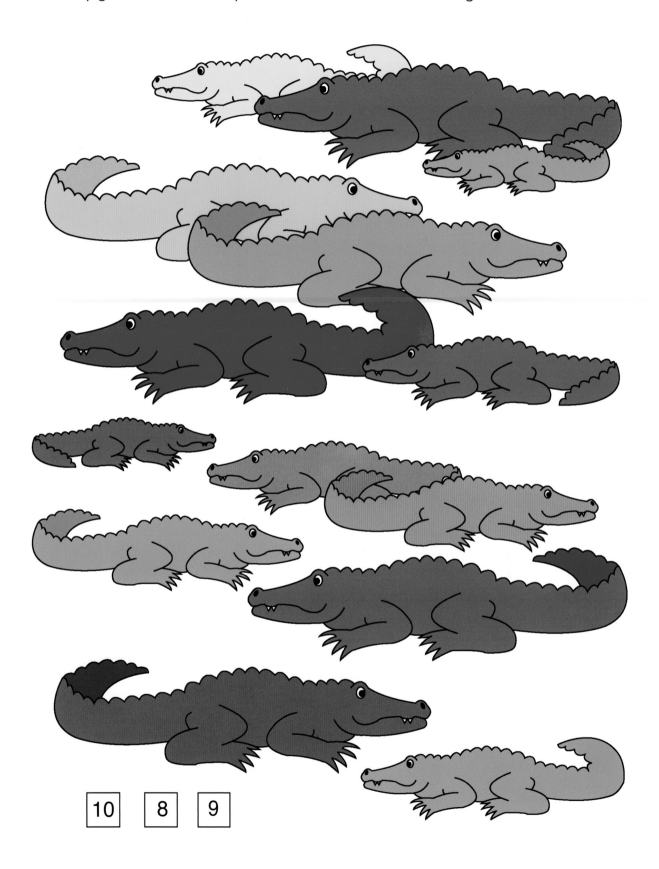

| 10 | 8 | 9 |

Can You Canoe?

Every canoe on this page has a twin that is almost the same. Find the twin for each canoe and connect them with a line.

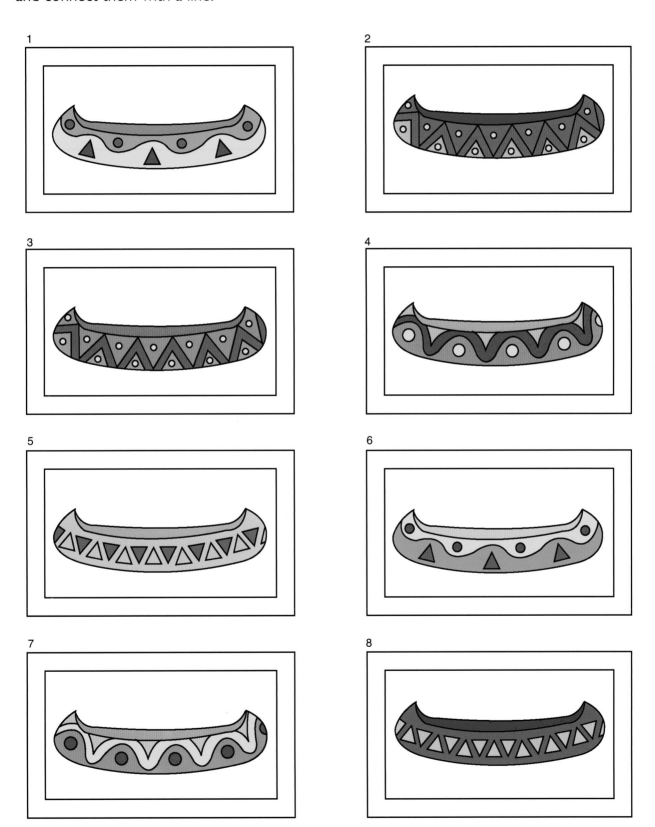

Animal Signs

On this table there are many colorful drawings. Circle all the animals you see.

Wonderful Wheels

Every wheel on this page has a twin that is almost the same. Find the twins and connect them with a line.

Teepee Town

All the teepees here look alike, except one. Find it and circle it.

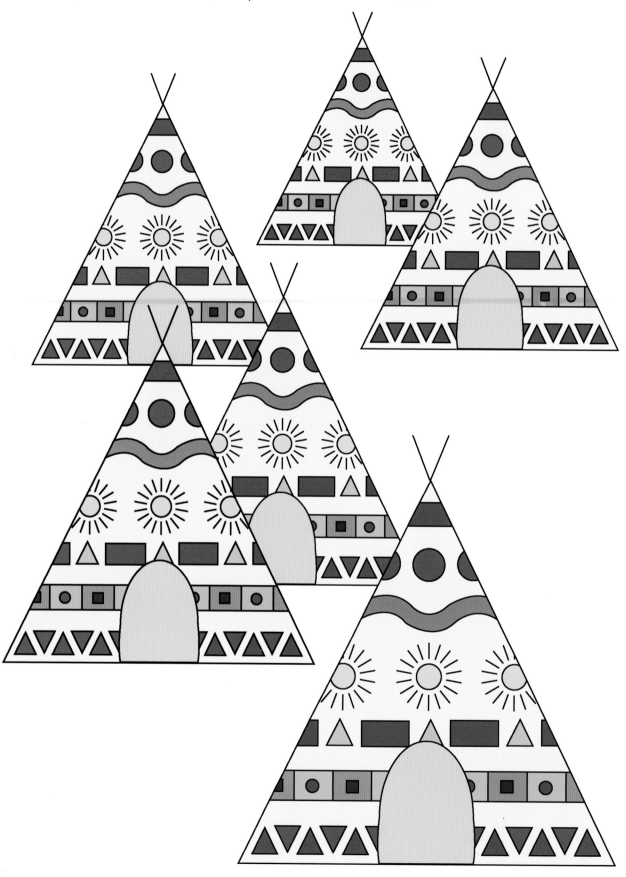

How Many Animals?

How many yellow snakes?

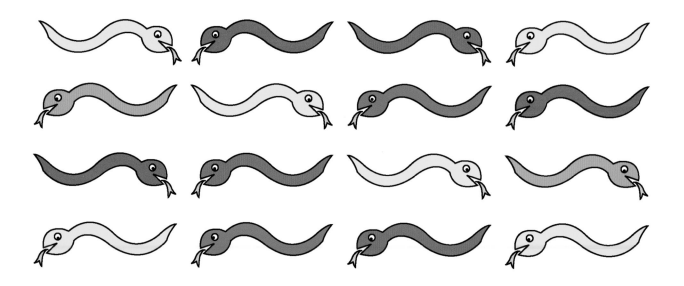

How many more fish, like the one in the small box?

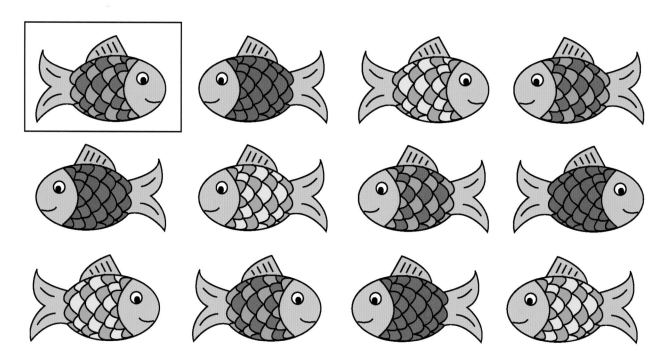

How many more turtles, like the one in the small box?

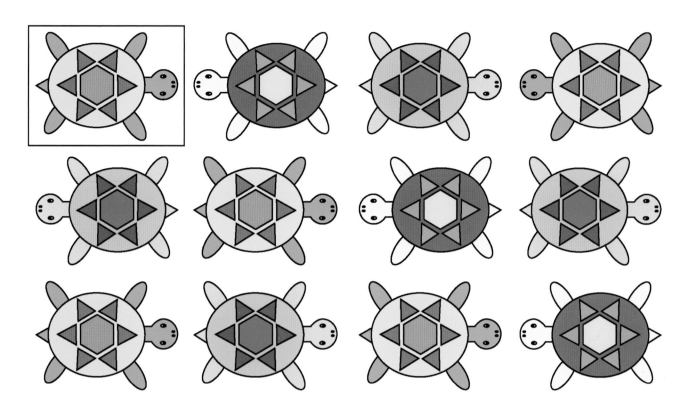

How many more crocodiles, like the one in the small box? (Pay attention to the direction of the tail.)

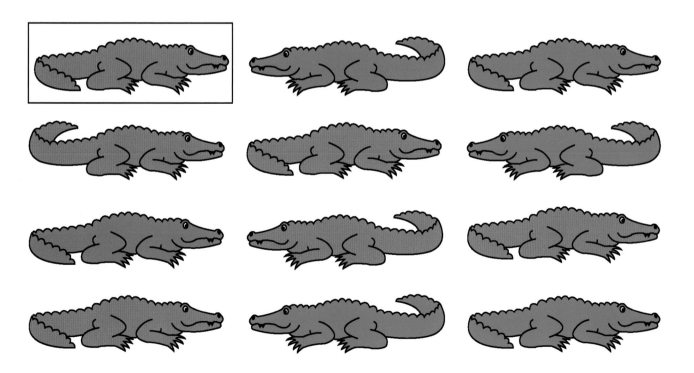

Ribbons of Suns

Each sun design in the square box is repeated in the ribbon that follows it. Circle each identical sun. How many are there in each ribbon?

Number Play

Find the number 7 and circle it. How many 7s are there?

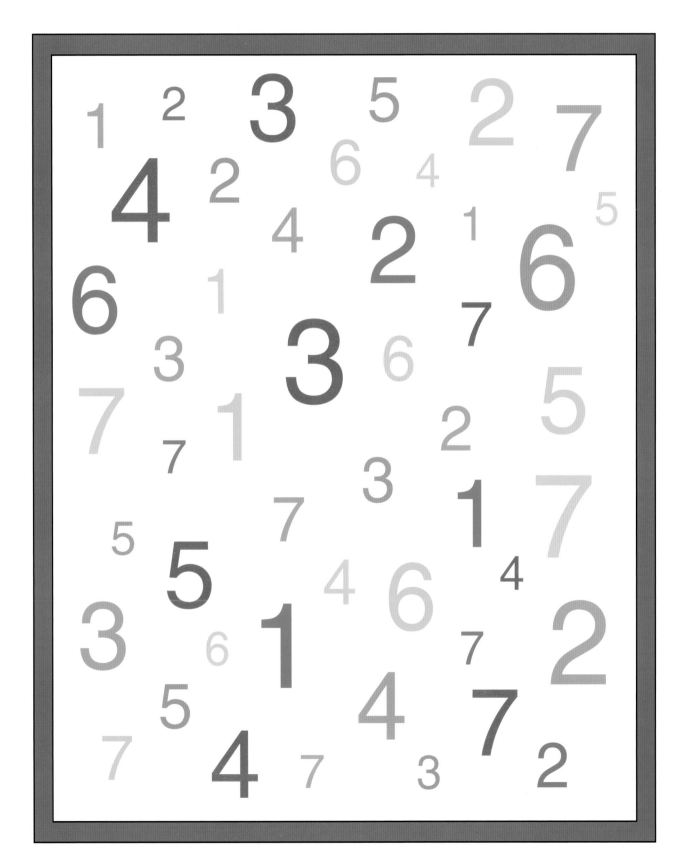

Nutty for Numbers

Look for all the shapes with a 2 in them and circle them. How many 2s are there on these pages?

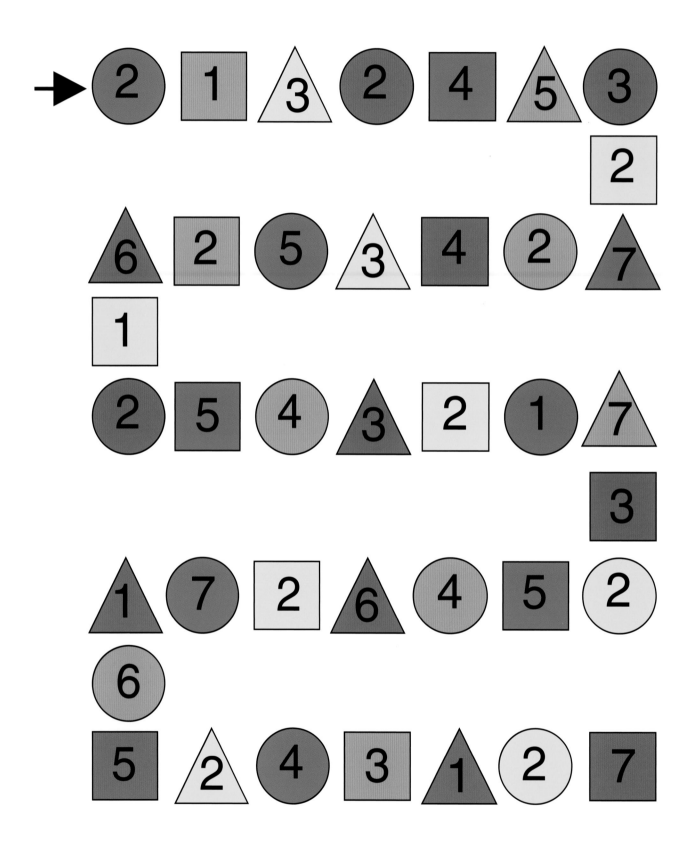

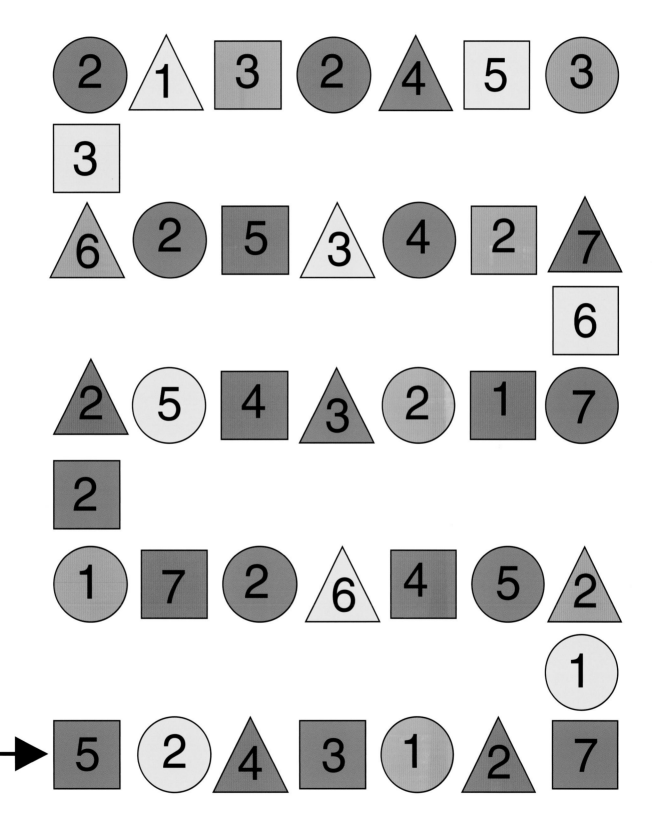

Red Triangles

Look for all the red triangles and circle them. How many are there?

Sharp Shapes

Look for the shape in the small box and circle it every time you see it. How many times does it appear?

Green Rectangles

Look for all the green rectangles. A rectangle is a shape that has 4 sides. Circle every green rectangle that you see. How many are there?

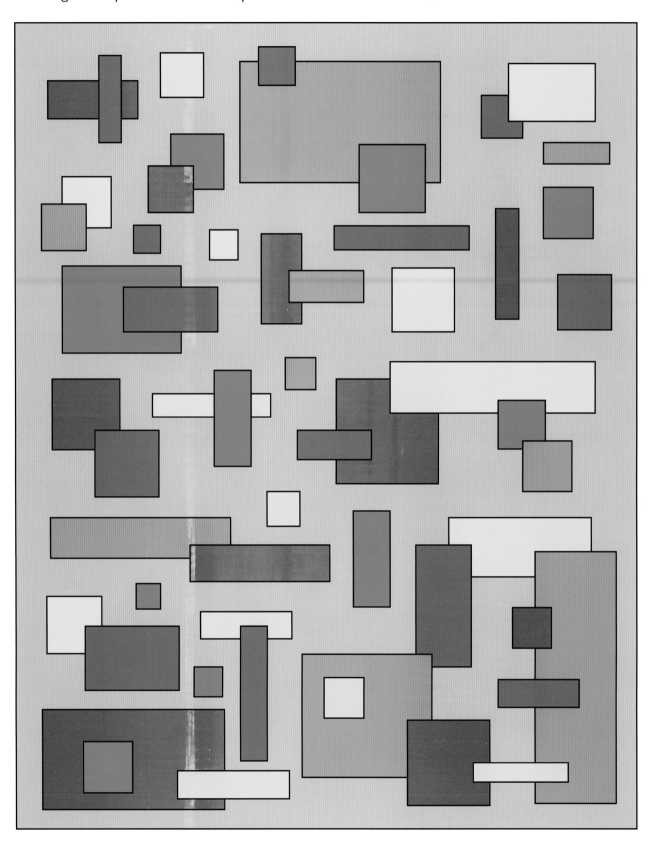

Play Ball #1

Look at the balls and memorize the colors and the way they change. See if you can find a good way to remember them. Then turn the page.

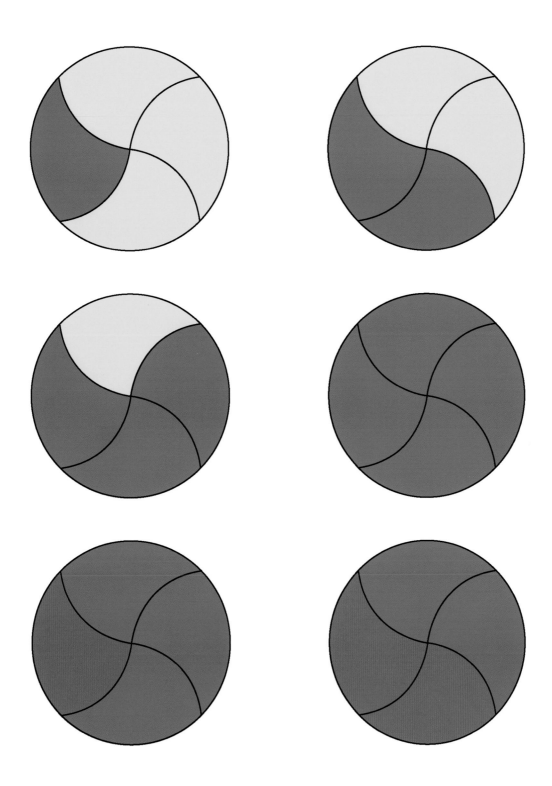

Play Ball #2

Check off the balls that you memorized. Then compare them with page 23.
How did you do?

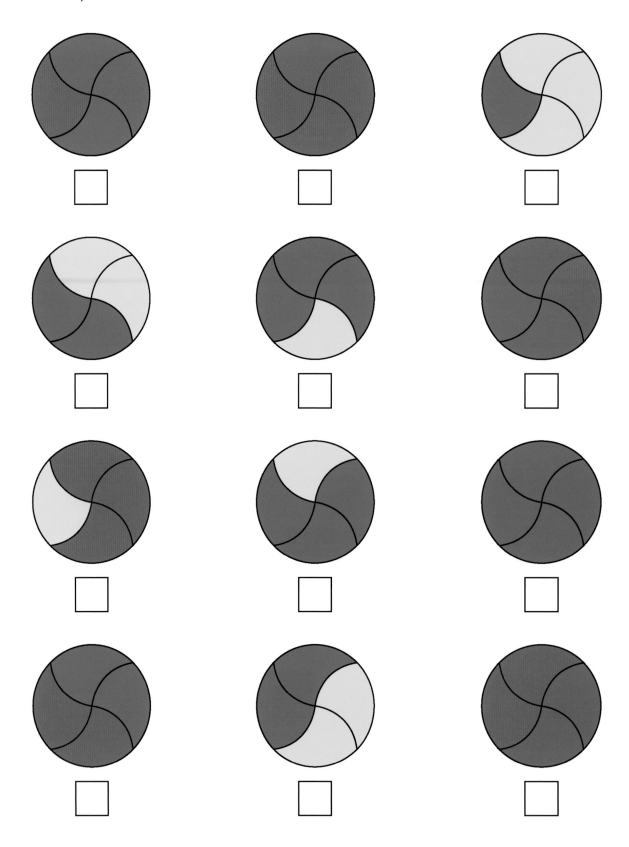

Test Your Memory

You can use colored pencils or crayons for this test. Memorize the shapes and colors in the first row. Then cover them up and draw the same shapes in the right colors in the row underneath. Can you do the same thing with the other rows?

Terrific Turtles

Each big turtle on this page has several little turtles exactly like it on page 27. Count them and write the number you find in the little sign beside each big turtle.

Memory Test

You'll need your colored pencils or crayons for this one.

Memorize the pattern on the upper left. Then cover it up and draw it in the box next to it in the right colors. Can you also do this with the other patterns?

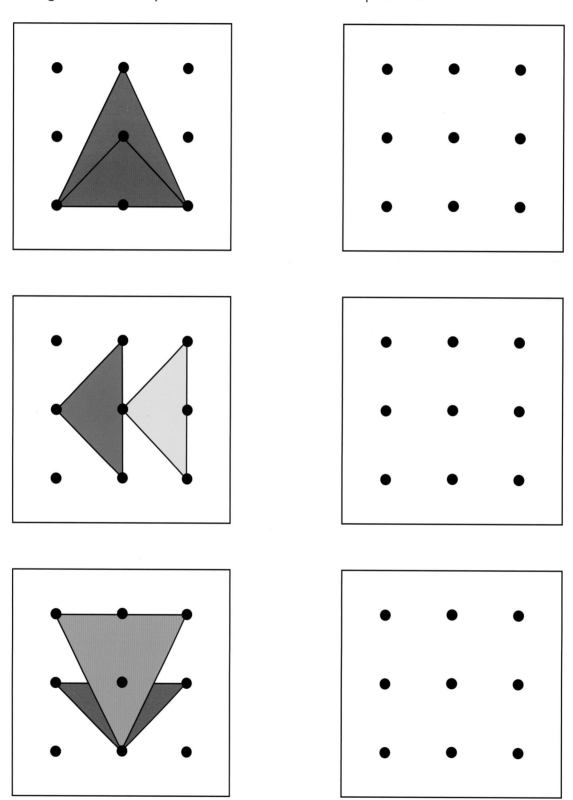

A Tricky Pattern

You'll need your colored pencils or crayons for this one too. Look carefully at the pattern. Copy it onto the empty grid below and color it in exactly.

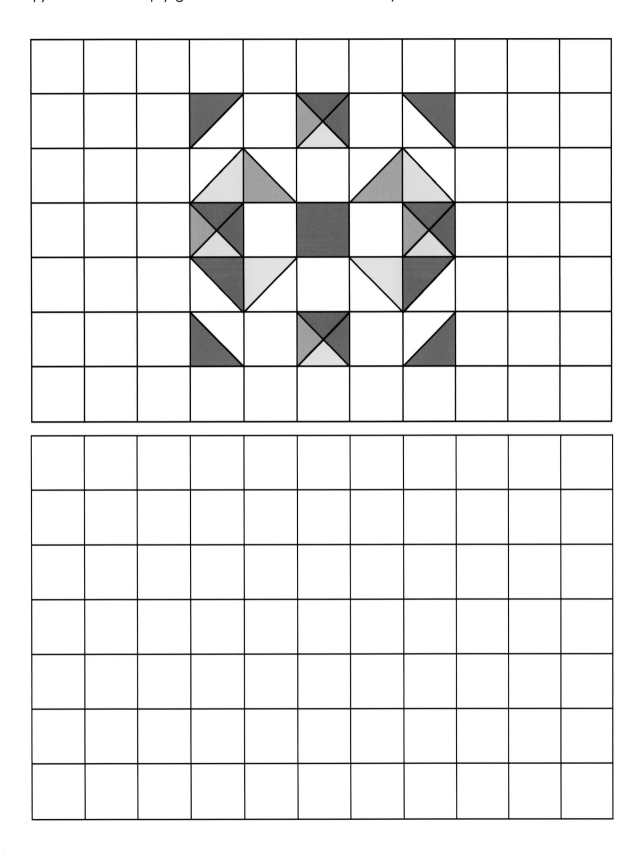

Butterflies

These butterflies come from 5 different families. Each family has a different color and design. Find the two butterflies that come from the same family and write the correct number in the little flower.

Numbers and Symbols

Each symbol has a number. Write the correct number in all the symbols in the square below.

Animals in Hiding

Other owls — just like the one in the box—are hiding in the owl lineup. Look at the rows carefully and find the identical owls. Circle them. How many identical owls are there?

Can you do the same thing for the rabbit and the fox?

Letter Squares

Oops! A mistake has crept into each one of these 4 squares. Can you find it and put a line through it?

A	N	V
N	A	V
W	N	A

E	F	T
T	L	E
F	E	T

D	B	G
G	B	C
B	D	G

O	P	S
S	K	O
P	S	O

Mama!

You can write MAMA twice with these letter cubes. Look for the right cubes and connect them with lines. Use each cube only once.

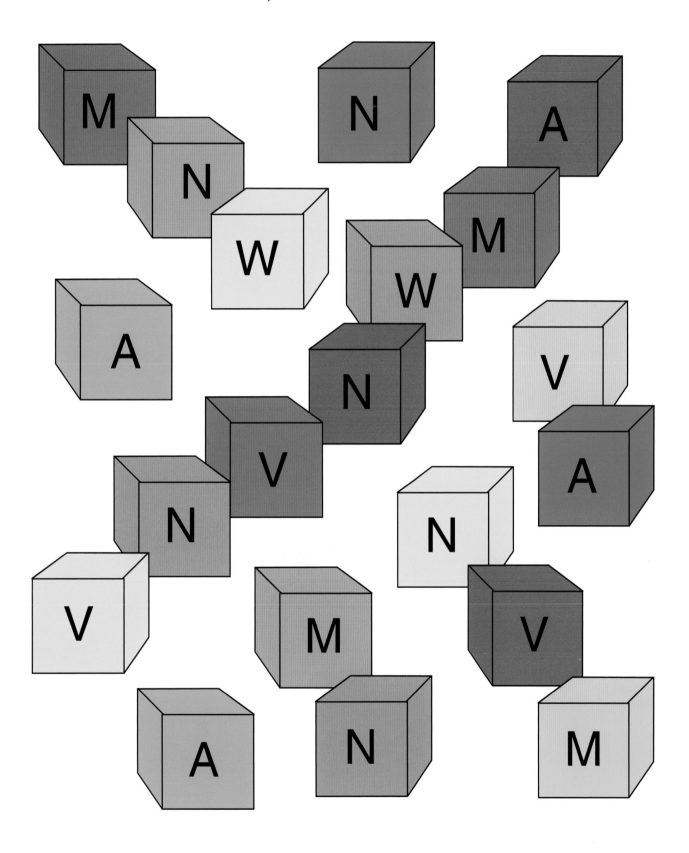

Letter Rows

Look carefully at the top 3 rows of letters and search for the letter in the small box — the N. Circle every N in the 3 rows. How often does it appear?

Do the same thing for the E, the K, and the G. How often do they appear?

N

```
A D C M N E K L N A W E
E R B N J F R S W N U O
W E N J K N R Q U M N A
```

E

```
K L F O N E K L G A W E
E R B E M P R S E N U O
R E N J K N E R U M N E
```

K

```
L D C M K E K L N U W K
E K B N J F P S W T U M
N K R J H N K Q V M L B
```

G

```
U D G M N K G L N A N E
L R B G J F G S W N Q M
H G N S K N H G U B P X
```

Playing Dice

The first die on the left shows the result. Circle the dice that are needed to come up with this result.

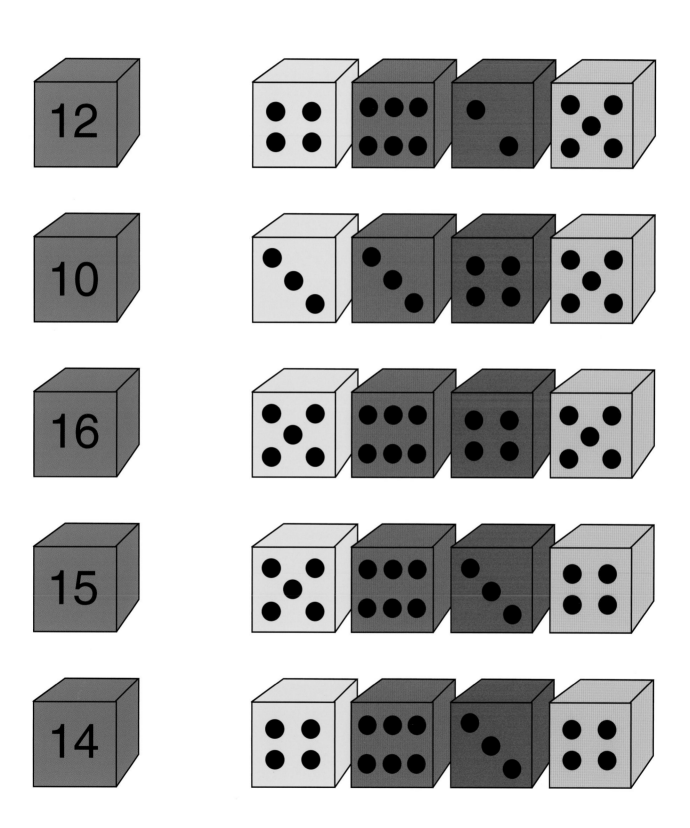

Cute Cubes

These cubes each have a twin — well, almost a twin. A mistake has crept into each pair.
First match up the twin cubes and draw a line connecting them. Then find the mistake and
circle it!

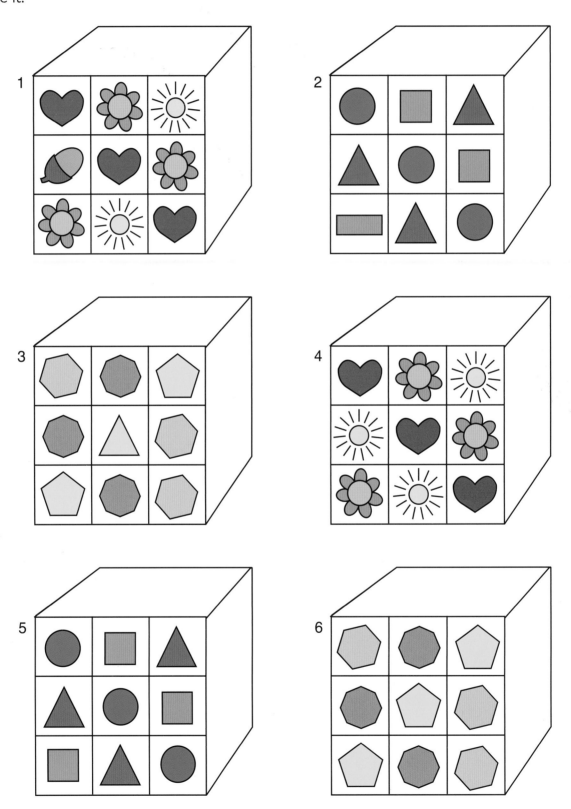

Snail Search

Look for the 4 snails in the box and circle them. How many of each one can you find?

The Number House

Look at the Number House and cross out the numbers from 1 to 30.

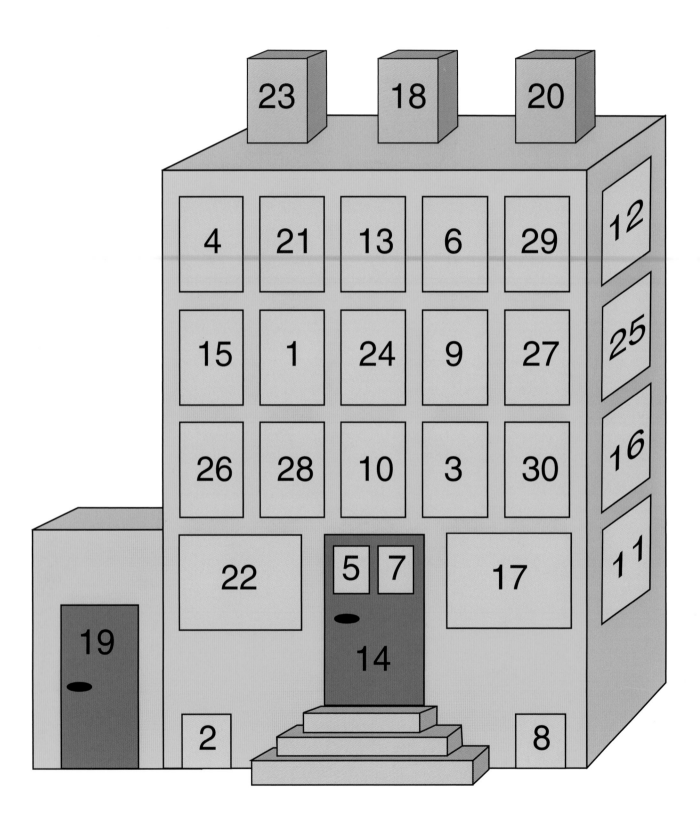

Crossing the Circles

The picture is made up of a lot of circles. Count them and put a check next to the right number shown below.

21		22		19	

The Letter Tree

The letters have gotten completely mixed up with each other. Follow the letters with your finger, starting with A and going through the alphabet to Z. Are they all there?

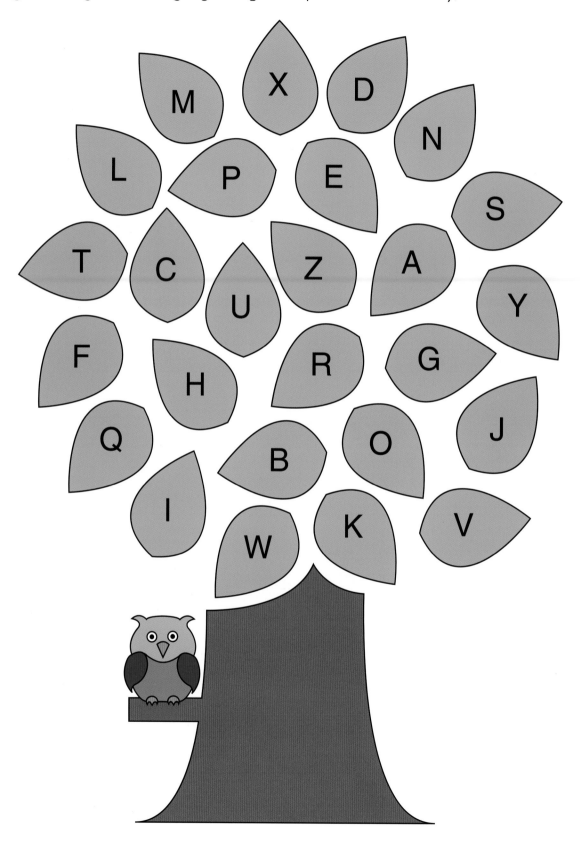

The Number Castle

Quickly indicate with your right index finger all the numbers that have one or more 5s in them. How many are there?

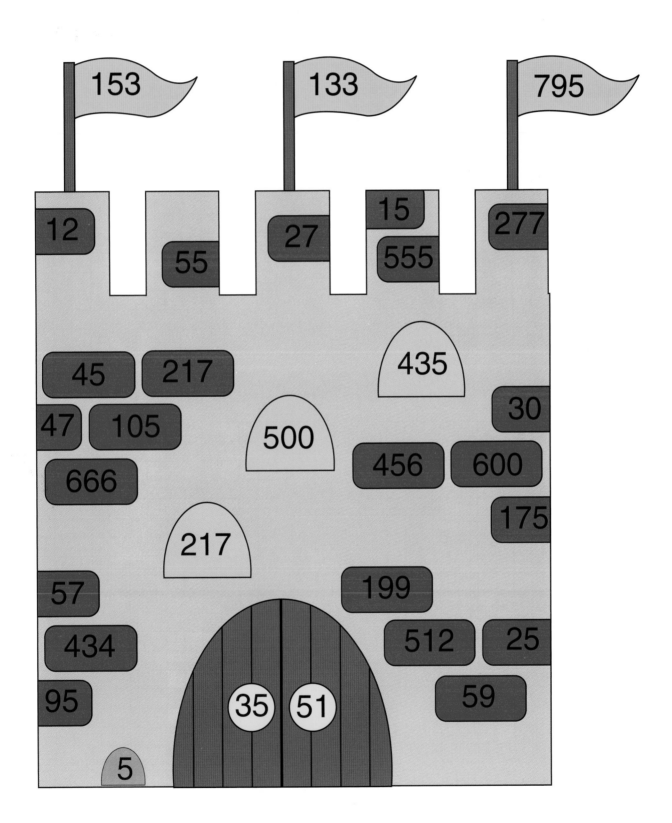

Letter Grids

How many letters are in each grid? In this puzzle, all the boxes that make up a letter are in one color. Write the answer in the little box under the grid.

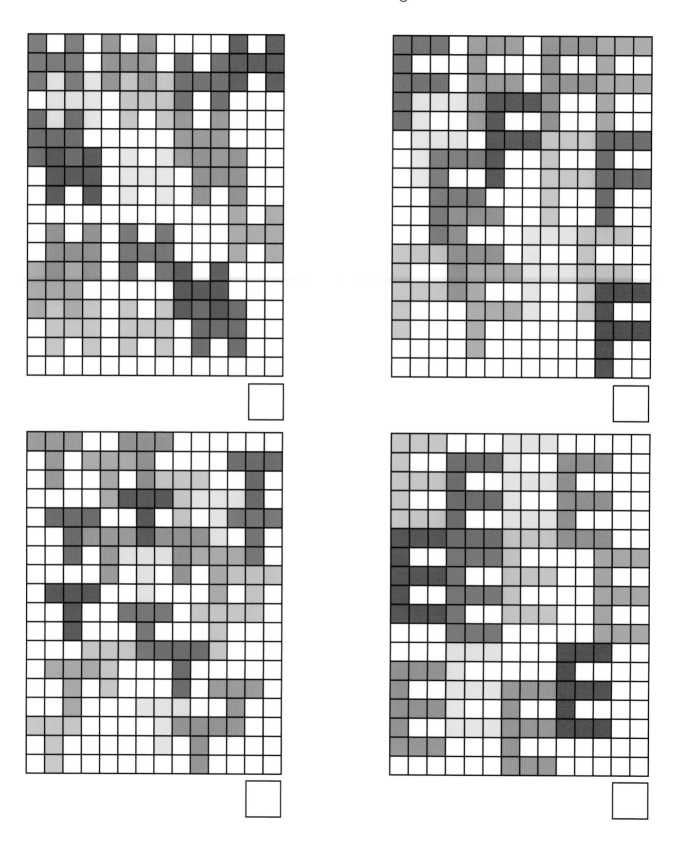

Squares and Cubes

How many squares or cubes can you find in this picture? Use a pencil to help count them.

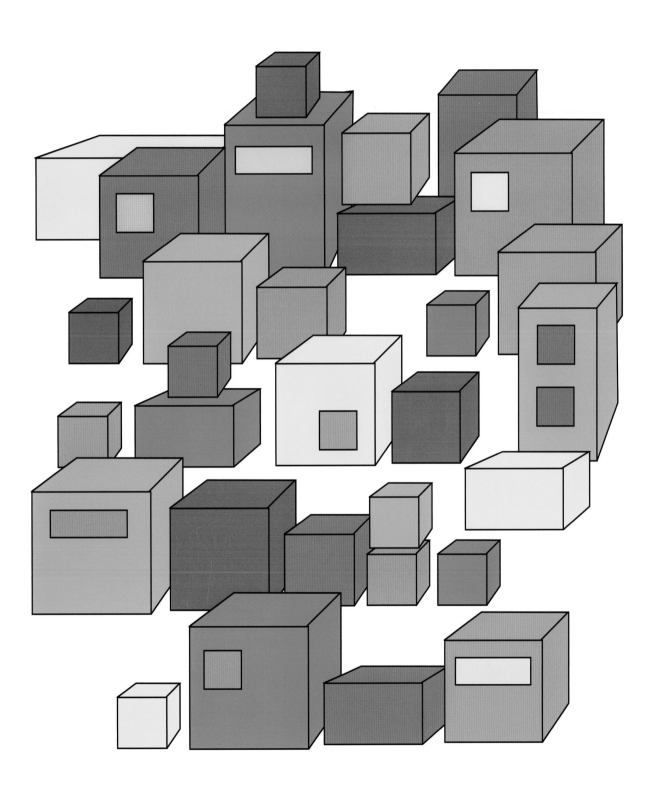

How Many What's-Its?

You'll find different objects in these circles, but what they are doesn't matter. Two of each circle have the same number of things in them. Can you match up the circles with the same number of what's-its — and tell what they are?

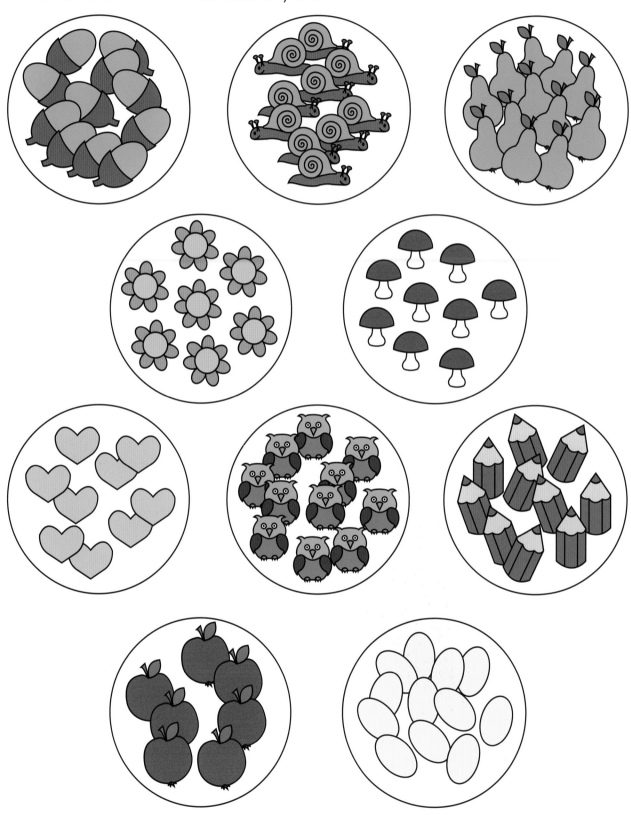

Mirror Numbers

On the left you see numbers as they would look in the mirror. Write them correctly in the yellow boxes.

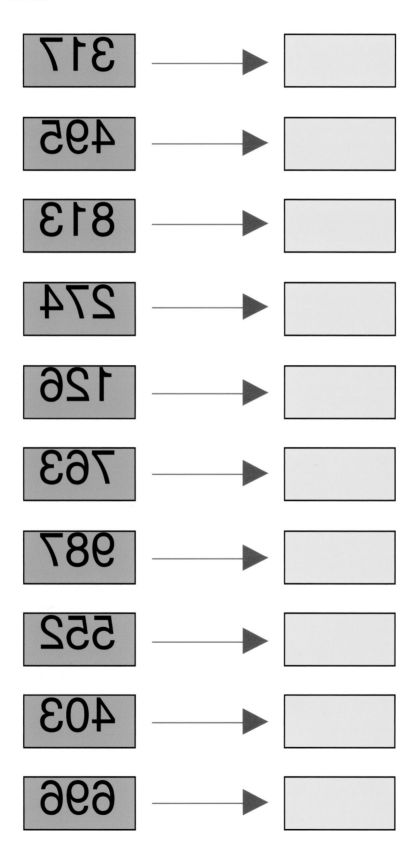

Count the Shapes

There are many different shapes in this picture. Count the rectangles, circles, and triangles, and write the number of each in the small boxes below.

Find the Letters

Here and there, letters have been placed between the symbols.
Find them and underline them.

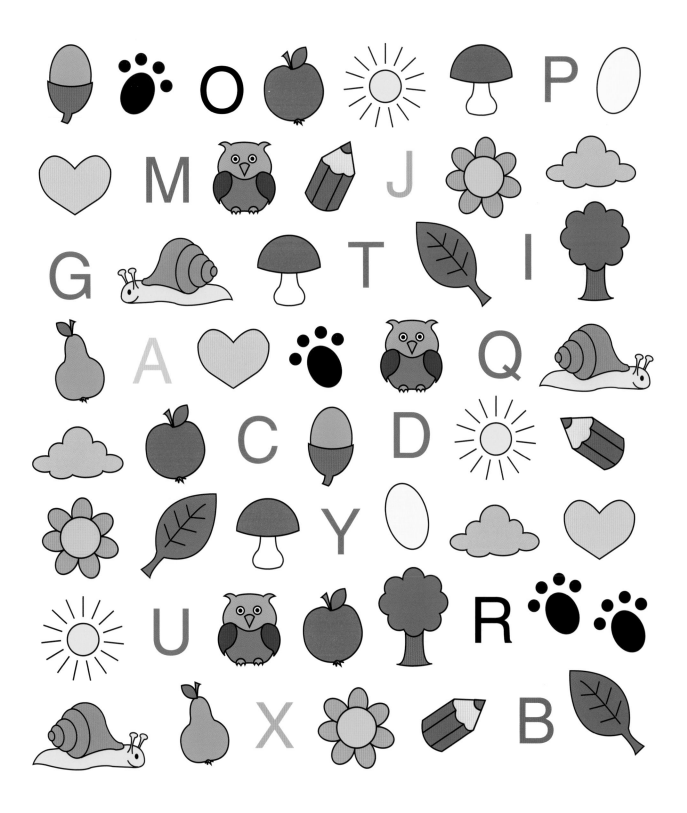

Puzzle Pieces

Which piece fits in the blank space — A, B, or C? Find the right puzzle piece and write its letter in the small box below the puzzle!

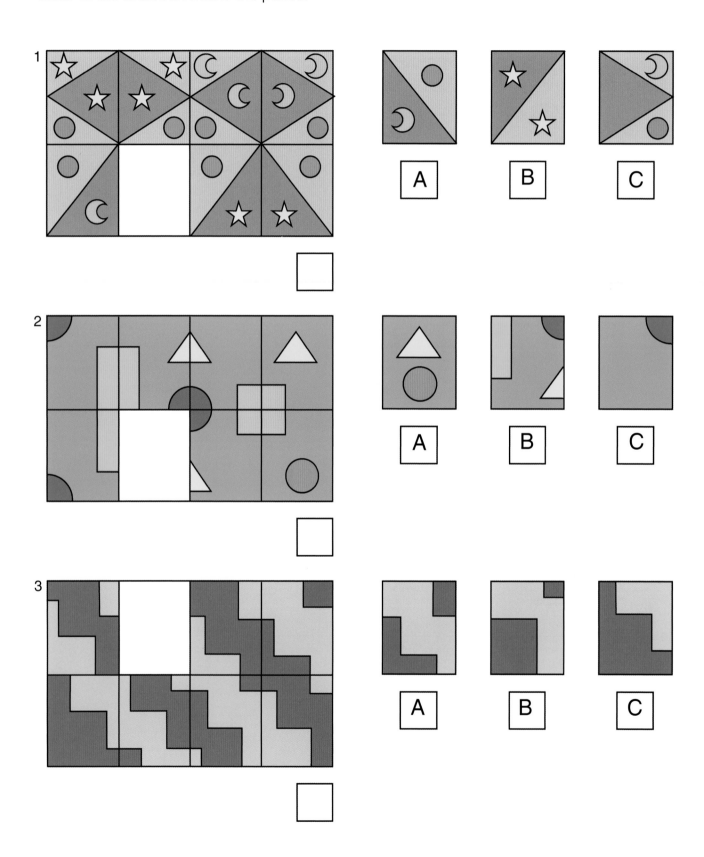

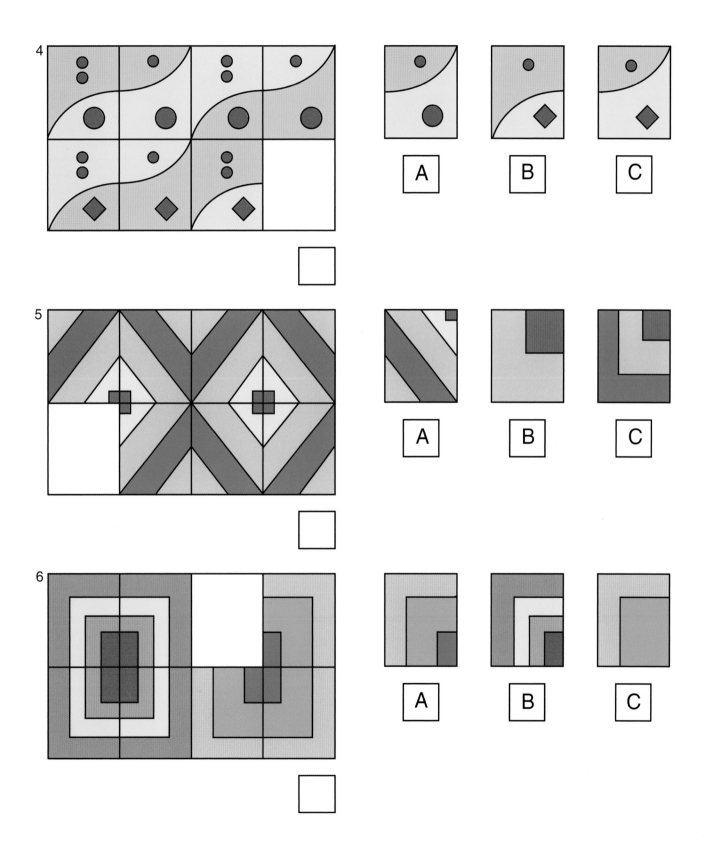

4

A B C

5

A B C

6

A B C

51

What Happens Next?

Which drawing comes next—A or B?
Continue the rows, and write your answer in the circle under your choice.

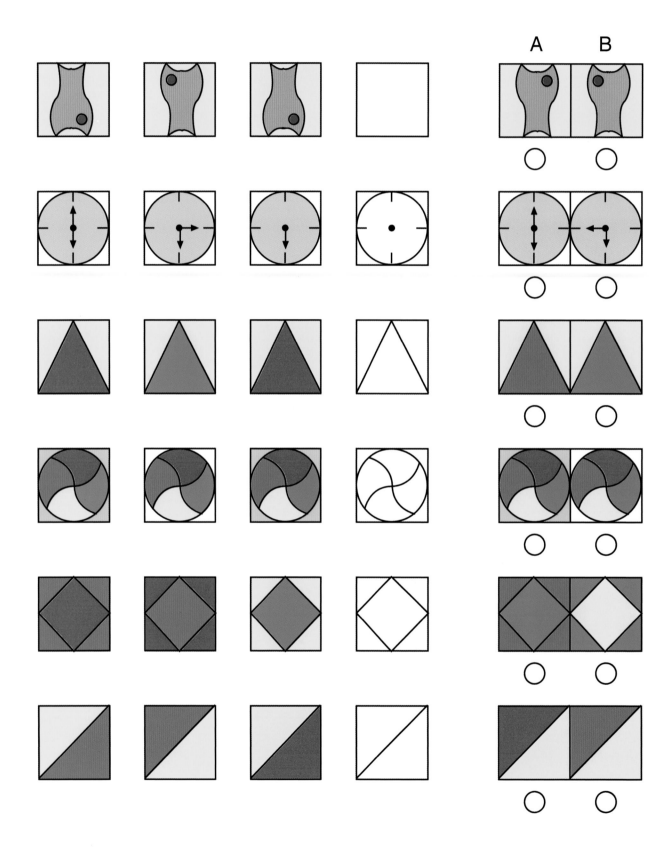

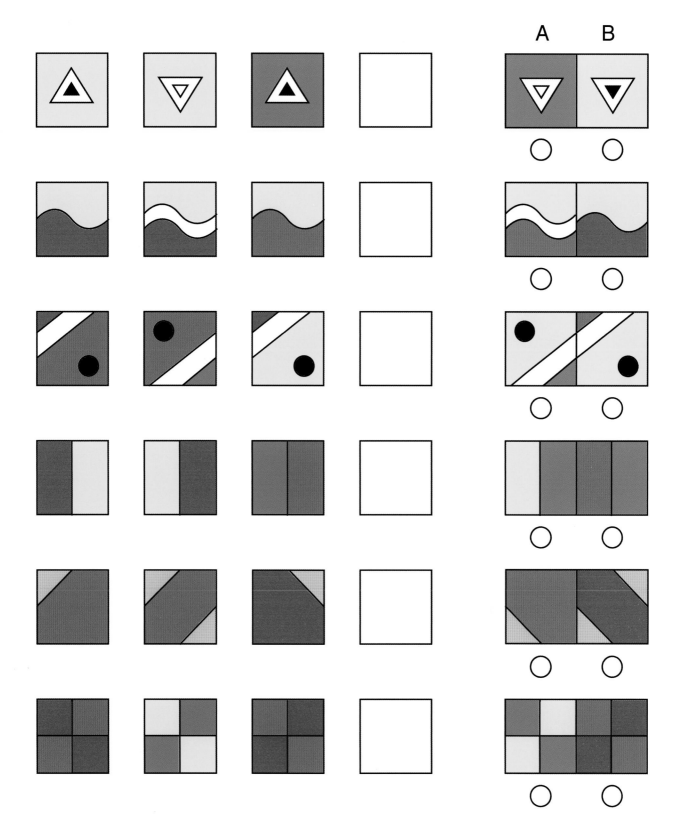

Flags

Here you see many flags with different designs. Each one has a matching circle on the next page. Write down the right number in the box beside the flag.

Which Picture Doesn't Belong?

All the objects in a row belong together — except for one that doesn't fit. Can you find the one that's out of place — and circle it?

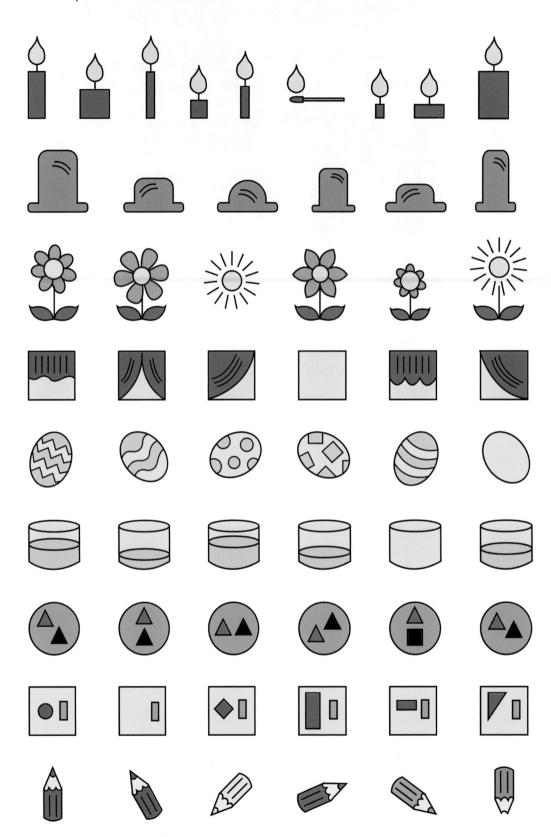

Dominoes

The dominoes lie in a certain order. Can you tell what it is? Which one comes next? Choose it, and check the circle underneath.

Complete the Picture!

In each picture frame a sign is missing. Which one — A, B, or C? Choose the picture that belongs and put down the right letter in the empty box!

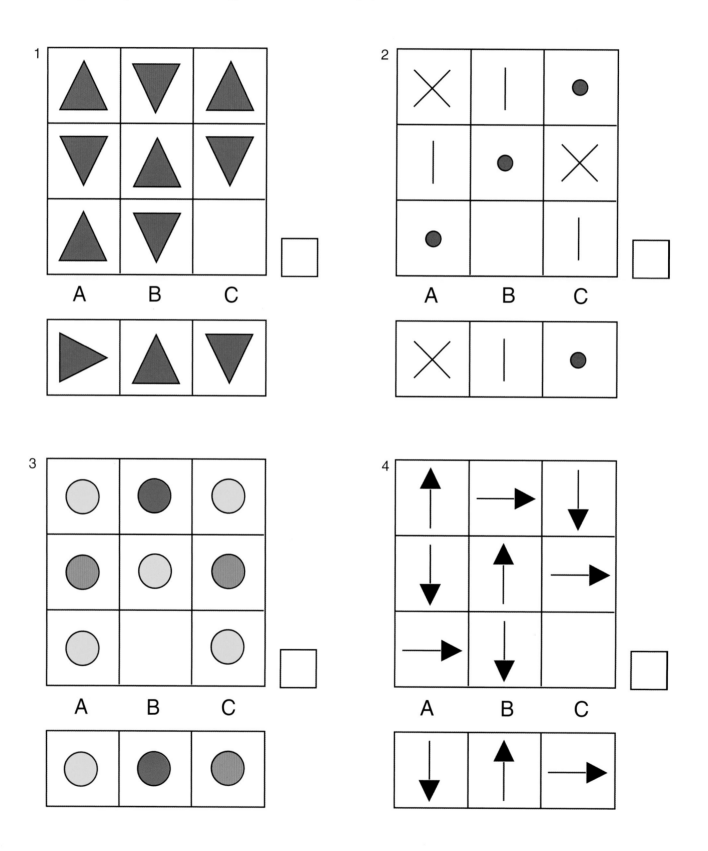

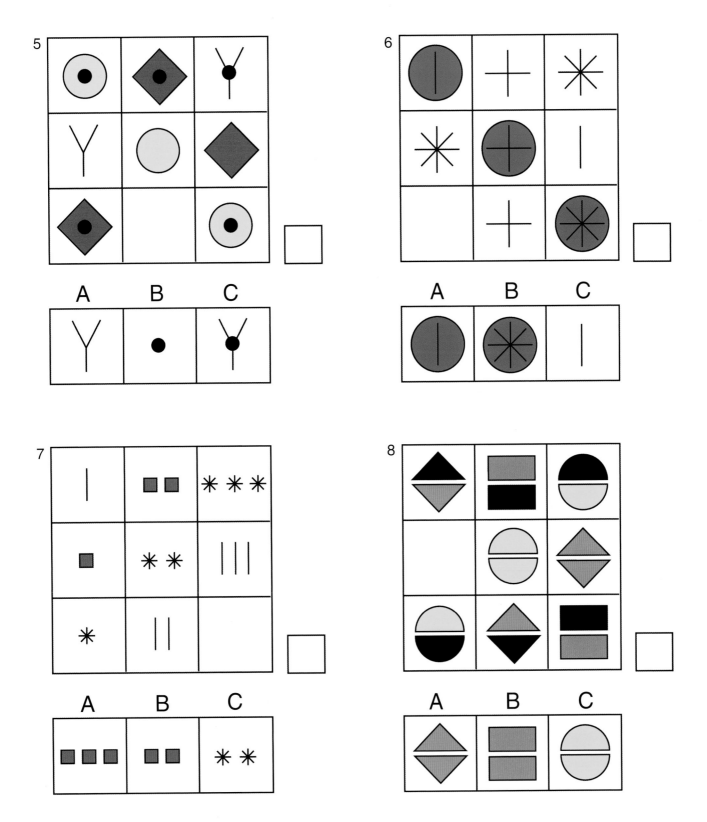

Shapes

If you put together the shapes in each box on this page, what shape would you get? Match up the shapes with the pictures on page 61 and write your answers in the empty box.

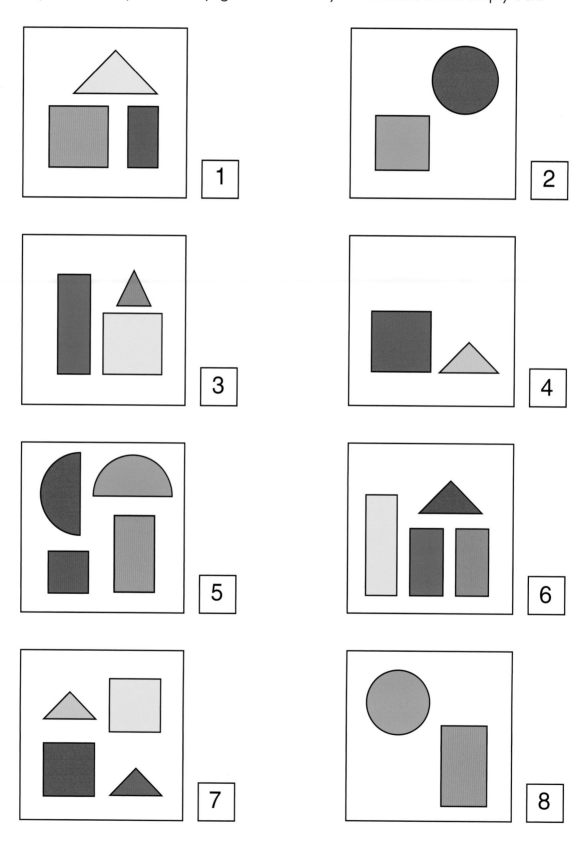

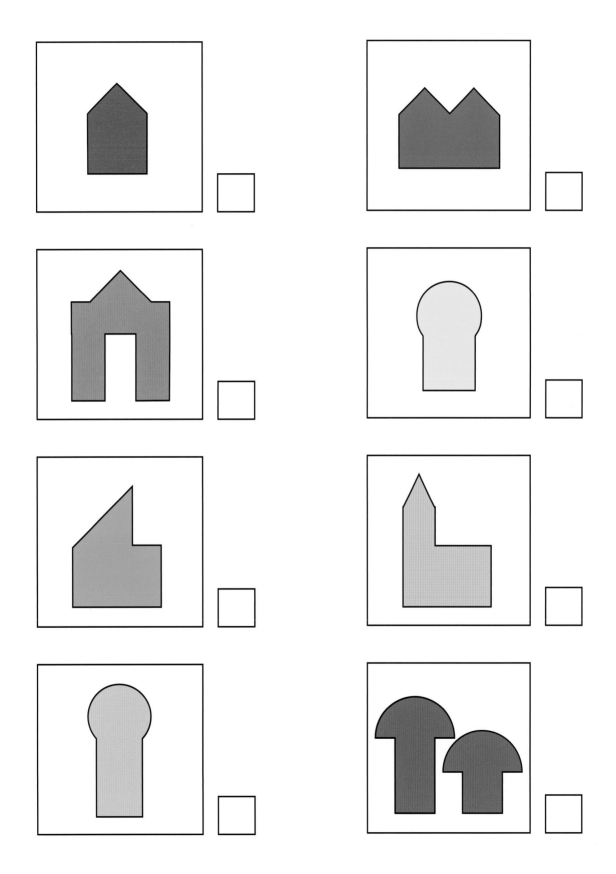

Broken Jugs

What kind of container do you get when you put the pieces back together? Write your answer in the empty box.

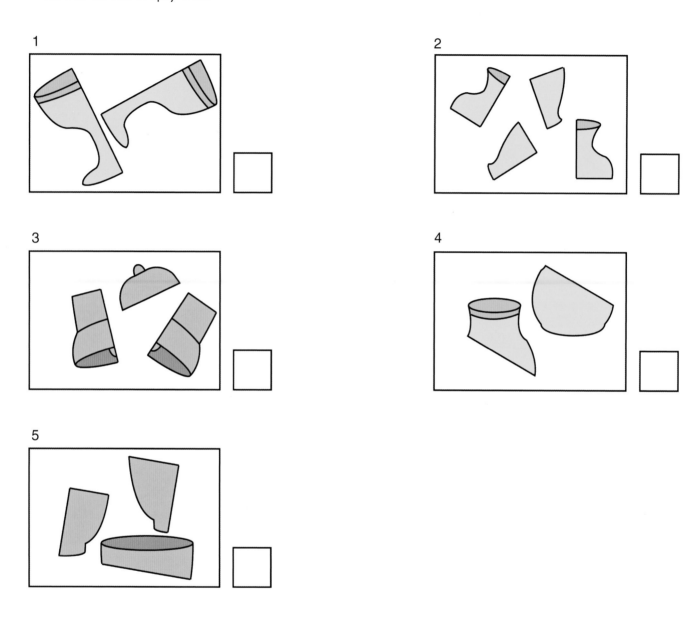

1

2

3

4

5

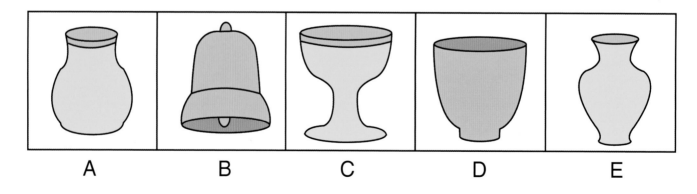

A   B   C   D   E

In the City #1

Memorize what the houses look like. Then memorize the vehicles that are in the parking lot! And wait for "In the City #2," the second part of this memory test.

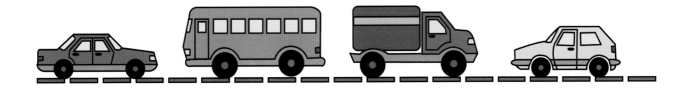

Mirror Images

If the line dividing each box on this page were a mirror, what would you see? Find the right mirror image on the next page and put its letter in the empty box.

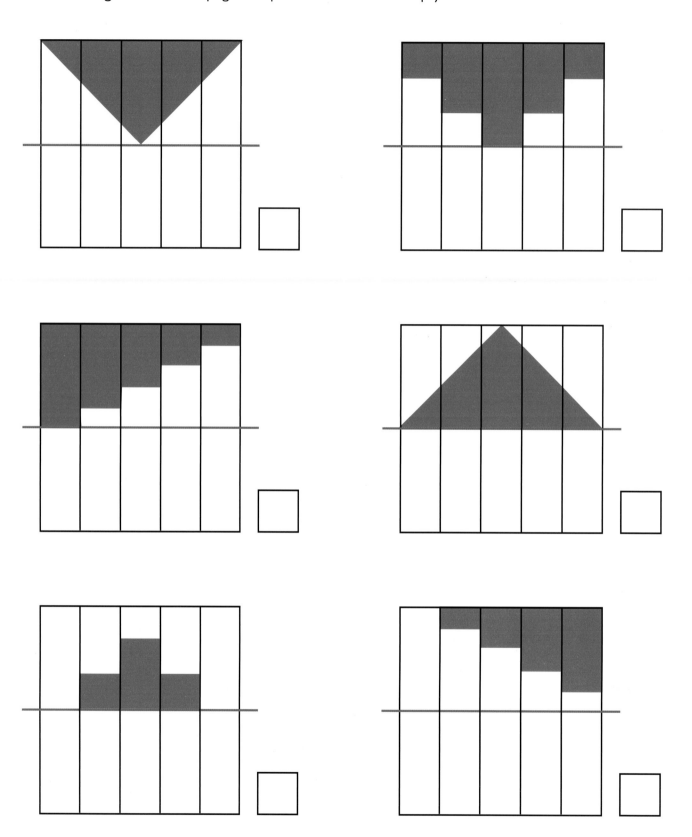

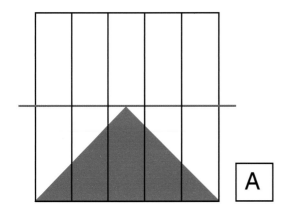

A

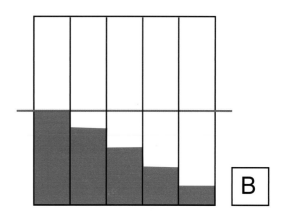

B

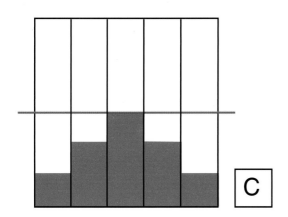

C

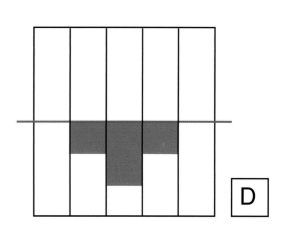

D

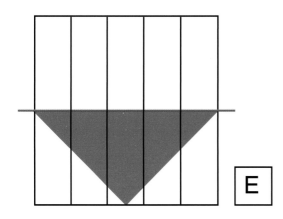

E

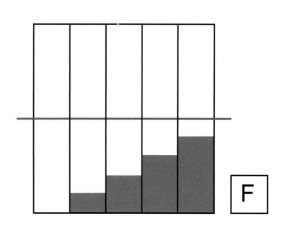

F

Fruit Salad

Every picture on this page appears on page 67, too, but it is flip-flopped. Can you find the pictures that are the same? Write your answers in the small boxes beneath the flopped pictures.

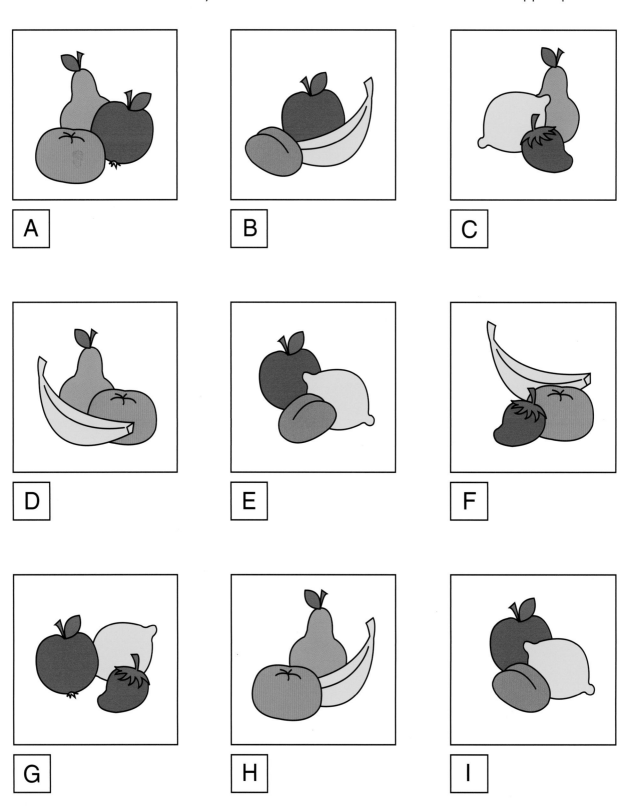

A

B

C

D

E

F

G

H

I

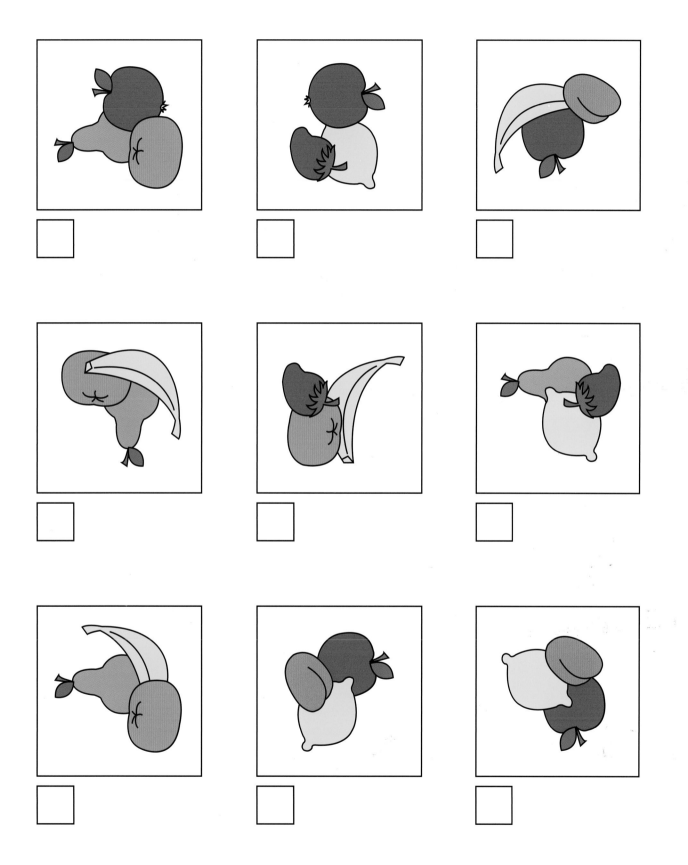

In the City #2

Remember that you memorized some of these houses and vehicles on an earlier page? Here is your chance to test your memory. Check off the ones you recognize in the empty box beneath them. Then compare them with page 63. Were you right?

Memorizing Patterns #1

The drawings on this page are all a little different from each other. Memorize how each pattern looks. You'll find the second part of this puzzle later on.

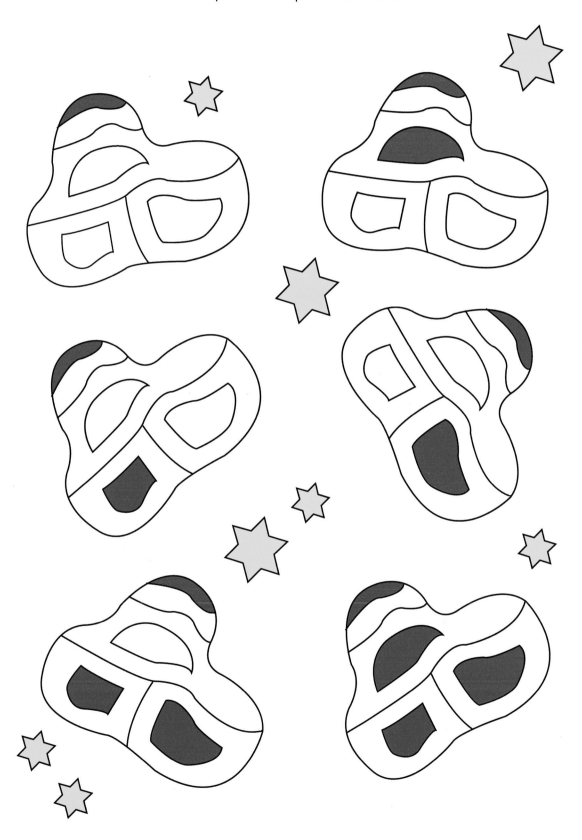

Mosaics

The pictures on this page are like pieces of a mosaic. Put them together. What kind of picture do you get? Find it on page 71, and write your answer in the small empty box.

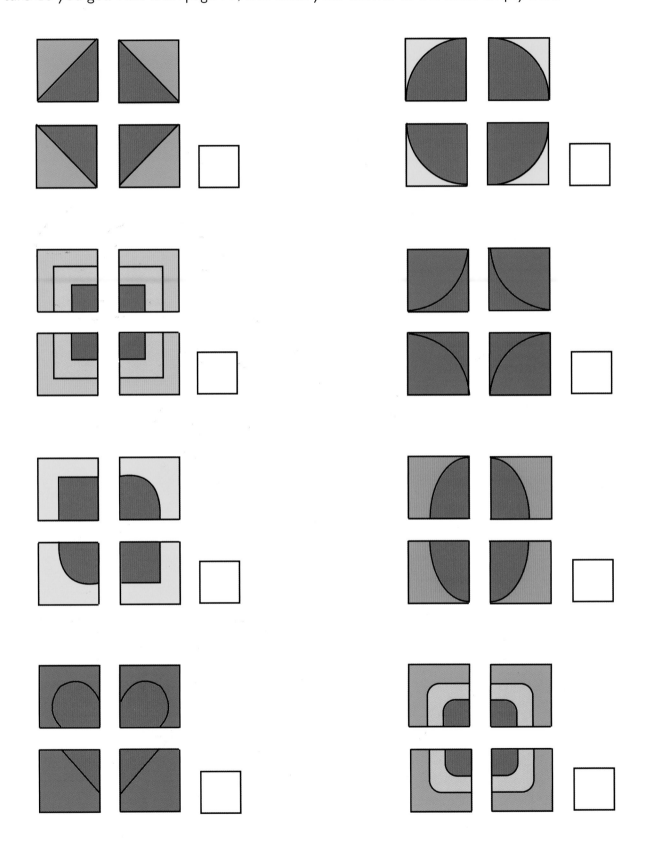

Memorizing Patterns 2

Do you recognize these patterns? What is missing? Use your crayons or colored pencils so that they look like the ones you memorized before. Then turn back to page 69 to see if you're right.

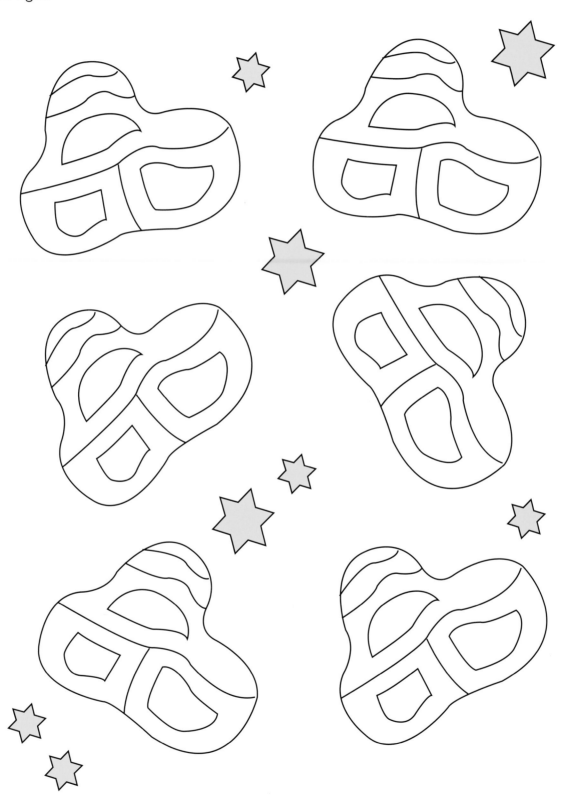

Pictures Instead of Numbers

Each shape is worth a different number of points. Can you keep track of these numbers while you add up the rows of shapes in your head? What results do you come up with? Write your answers in the empty box at the end of the row.

$\bullet = 1 \qquad \square = 2 \qquad \triangle = 3$

1. $\bullet + \triangle + \triangle + \bullet + \square + \square + \bullet = \boxed{}$

2. $\square + \triangle + \square + \triangle + \bullet + \triangle + \bullet = \boxed{}$

3. $\triangle + \bullet + \square + \triangle + \bullet + \square + \triangle = \boxed{}$

4. $\bullet + \triangle + \bullet + \triangle + \bullet + \triangle + \bullet = \boxed{}$

5. $\square + \bullet + \bullet + \triangle + \bullet + \bullet + \square = \boxed{}$

6. $\bullet + \square + \square + \triangle + \bullet + \square + \triangle = \boxed{}$

Bite Out of the Apple

What part is missing? Can you match up the apple with the bite on the next page? Write your answer in the empty box under the bite.

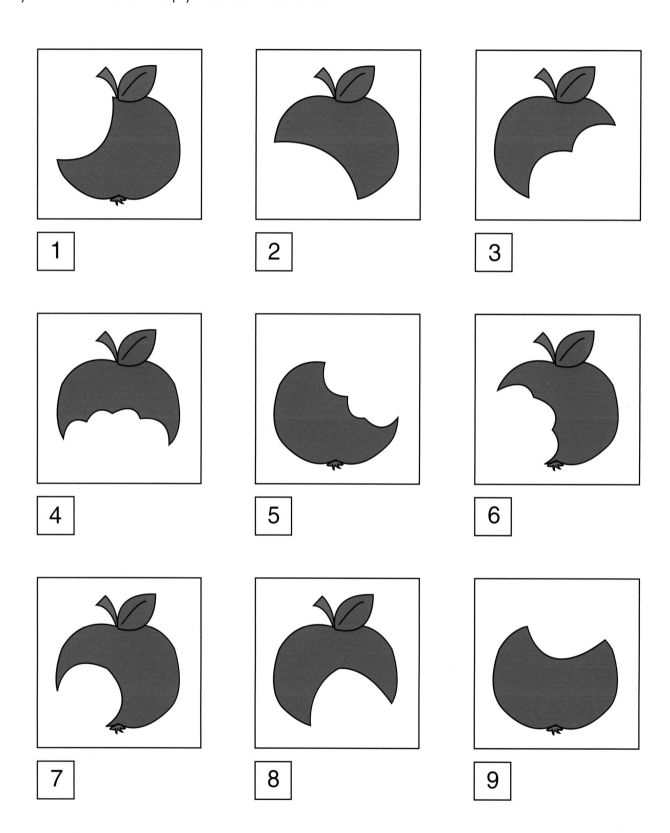

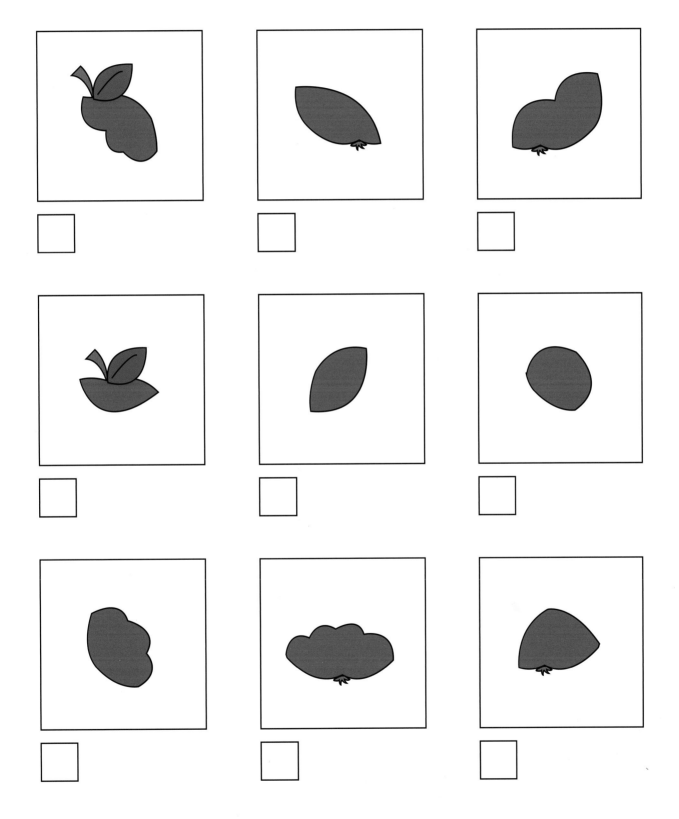

Recognizing Numbers

Look for the number in the first box and circle it. How often does each appear?

312	342	312	231	512	312
	321	412	312	312	234

987	789	987	798	987	897
	987	879	789	798	987

4231	4312	2413	4231	4231
	4123	4231	4312	1324

6879	7869	6879	9876	6879
	9876	8769	6879	6897

Solutions

Page 4:

Page 5: There are 18 complete circles.

Page 6-7: The eagle from the small box is repeated 3 times.

Page 8: There are 8 green crocodiles.

Page 9: Canoes 1 and 6, 2 and 3, 4 and 7, and 5 and 8 are almost alike.

Page 10:

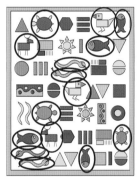

Page 11: Wheels 1 and 6, 2 and 4, 3 and 8, and 5 and 7 are almost alike.

Page 12-13:

Page 14-15: The snake appears 6 times.
The fish appears 3 more times.
The turtle appears 4 more times.
The crocodile appears 3 more times.

Page 16: The first sun appears 6 times, the second sun 5 times and the third sun 5 times.

Page 17: The number 7 appears 10 times.

Page 18-19: The number 2 comes up 22 times.

Page 20: There are 12 red triangles.

Page 21: The shape in the box appears 10 times more.

Page 22: There are 10 green rectangles.

Page 26-27:

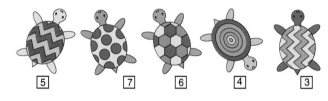

Page 30-31:

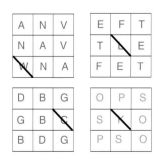

Page 33: The owl, hare, and fox each appear 3 times more.

Page 34:

Page 35:

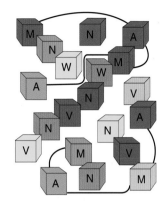

Page 36: The N is there 7 times, the E 8 times, the K 6 times, and the G also 6 times.

Page 37:

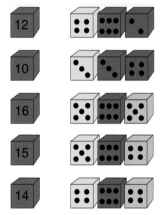

Page 38: 1 and 4 are almost the same (mistake:)

2 and 5 are almost the same (mistake:)

3 and 6 are almost the same (mistake:)

Page 39: The first snail is there 3 times, the second 3 times, the third 4 times, and the fourth 3 times.

Page 41: There are 22 circles.

Page 42: Yes they are!

Page 43: There are 20 numbers with a 5 in them.

Page 44: The H appears 19 times, the F 15 times, the T 24 times, and the E 12 times.

Page 45: Have you found all 28 rectangles?

Page 46: 11 acorns and owls
10 snails and colored pencils
12 pears and eggs
7 flowers and apples
9 mushrooms and hearts

Page 47: 317, 495, 813, 274, 126, 763, 987, 552, 403, 696

Page 48: 16 rectangles, 9 circles, 17 triangles

Page 49:

O, P, M, J, G, T, I, A, Q, C, D, Y, U, R, X, B

Page 50: 1A, 2B, 3A

Page 51: 4C, 5A, 6A

Page 52: from top to bottom:
B, B, B, B, B, A

Page 53: from top to bottom:
A, A, A, B, B, A

Page 54:

4		8
6		5
3		7
2		1

Page 56:

Page 57:

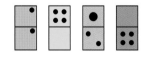